PLANNING FOR:

A REASON

A SEASON
&
A LIFETIME

By

Nicole B. Simpson, CFP

ISBN: 1-4107-1771-2 (e-book)
ISBN: 1-4107-1770-4 (Paperback)

Library of Congress Control Number: 2003090572

This book is printed on acid free paper.

Printed in the United States of America
Bloomington, IN

1stBooks – rev. 01/31/03

CONTENTS

Acknowledgments

Dear Heavenly Father,

I wanted to take this time to say thank you. I count it a privilege and honor that you have chosen to use me as a vessel. I do not take your charge and your mandate on my life for granted. I pray that everything I do is of you. Diminish me Lord and flow through me freely. I understand that my divine purpose is to do your will. Let my light shine so that men might see your good works. Whatever it is that you call for me to do, I am willing and with you I am able. I understand that you have given me a Ministry of Finance. Please know that I am committed to using the gifts you have given me to ultimately lead people to Christ. Help me to let my life be an example of you. It is my desire that even when I don't speak about your good name, my attitude, my behavior, and my character all reflect someone attempting to walk with you. I surrender all to you. I know I cannot walk this journey alone and challenges will surround me always. But greater are you within me then he is within the world. I am excited about the new dimension you are bringing me to. I pray that I will not disappoint you in my walk to serve you. Be with me always. I will be careful to give you all of the glory. Without you I am nothing.

Your faithful servant,
Nicole

With special thanks:

To my husband Jesse,

I count is an honor and a privilege that you have chosen me to be your wife. Your constant support and advice helped me to be the woman I am today. The Bible states he who finds a wife, finds a good thing. I state today, I'm glad you found me. I love you and I could not picture my life with anyone else.

To my precious children Jesse and Emani,

I could never ask for more than what I already have in you. The two of you make it easy to get up each day. You are a Simpson and you represent your dad and me better than I could ever imagine. I love you and I thank God I have the cream of the crop with you.

Robert Krebs,

Many people in my life don't even know your name. Every major business decision I ever made, I've consulted you first. My success is your success as well. Your guidance, your support, and most importantly, your teachings contribute to my expertise as an advisor.

To Mom, Wilma,

Each day I am reminded of your words you stated so often. Look at my life as an example of what you should and should not do. Being half the woman you are would be all right with me. Please know that I love you and would not ask for anything to be different in my life.

Anita, Sonji, and Tonya; my sisters,

Growing up with you prepared me for the world. I have learned how to love, support, persevere, stay and fight, and walk away from every situation. You are the backbone of my strength. Thank you for being you.

Fayemi,

You make me look good. Your commitment to this project is a blessing. Thank you.

Imani Christian Fellowship,

I know that prayer changes things. Thank you for keeping me in your prayers. I thank God for such a supportive family.

I want to specifically thank others.

Simbell Riddick, Denise Brown, Sergeant DeLacy Davis, Vashti Encarcion, my mother-in-law Margaret Simpson, Reverend George M. Jones, my pastor, Sister Tonya Vines, Carlos "Shorty" Diaz, and Monique Smith of "Monique's Techniques".

PROLOGUE

When I turned thirty years old in January of 2001, I began to evaluate my life. I knew that God called me for a purpose and that purpose was to be a Minister of Finance. I did not know exactly what that meant, but I envisioned a young lady speaking to crowds of people teaching them about money. They would learn how to earn money, how to manage money, and ultimately how to keep money. That young lady would also serve to educate, empower, and enlighten the youth and the churches. Being that young lady, I knew that my culture needed economic empowerment.

As a minority, we finally have the resources and ability to make change in our community. However, we did not know how to get started. Hip Hop culture has given everyone the opportunity to think and grow rich. It also gave us the power we needed on a corporate level to make a significant difference if we chose to.

My knowledge and experience were there but what I envisioned and where I was at were two different places. My clientele as a certified financial planner consisted of mostly entertainers, corporate personnel, and small business owners. The picture of my calling was crystal clear. A change needed to be made to fulfill what God had called me to do.

At the age of thirty, I was in a partnership as a Certified Financial Planner and Financial Advisor at a major financial institution making over $100,000 a year working an average of seventy hours a week in an uncertain economy. I talked on the phone to clients all day. While I was on the phone, I was watching stocks and reading the latest news. If I wasn't doing business, I was meeting prospects and existing clients. I was also managing over $120 million in assets. Most of the clients in the partnership were not African American. And my partnership was not a true partnership. It was an unbalanced relationship. It was and is my desire to manage the same money with a majority of African American clients. I was having difficulty getting through to the very people I wanted so badly empower.

First of all, there aren't many African American Financial Advisors, let alone Certified Financial Planners. Most of the minority advisors in this business have a client roster that is predominantly white. To attempt to build a business with black clients is near impossible. To date, I've only heard about one other advisor in California that has been somewhat successful. Now I'm not saying there aren't many out there. Just after twelve years in the business, I don't know many. Most of the people I know gave up after six months because they really wanted to stay in the business. I do know a lot of advisors that have tried-without success. Sadly, I could speak with a new prospect and based on my credentials, that prospect could determine almost immediately if they were going to transfer their account to me. However, when dealing with minority prospects, it takes me almost three times as long to convert a new account I attribute that to the fact that there aren't enough minority experts in our field. It also supports the fact that minorities historically have not had exposure to the financial world, therefore how can one respect the qualifications of an expert. In the last few years, I've seen a rash of minority advisors being hired at boutique firms, mutual fund companies, and small investment banks. Someone realizes that there is wealth in our communities.

"What is holding me back from working with people of my culture?" I pondered. I believe the lack of financial knowledge in the minority community keep so many of us from getting ahead. That is why I originally felt the need to write this book. I believe this book will serve as a basic fundamental tool that will allow people to read experiences, ideas, and various client relationships that will help evaluate their own lives. This material is designed to make you think about your very own situations.

Unfortunately, often we look to entertainers or financial experts for overall advice. Because entertainers are often in the public eye, their lives are an open book. People relate to the experiences of their favorite artists or actors. Some of these stories are things that typically occur in the average family. Sometimes we will see events that may have affected our family, our friends, and our neighbors. But should we try to model our lifestyles and ways of living by the lives of these entertainers?

Seeing all too clearly the issues at hand, it was time to begin the work God wanted me to do. I began to write one week after turning thirty years old at my computer at home. I was very focused and committed to outlining new goals and objectives for myself. The book was coming along and I was dedicated to writing at least two times a week. I was relying on a disk to store my data and the information was saved in my computer on my job. After losing the data, which I will elaborate on later, I became very frustrated and I decided that a book was not in the cards for me.

In January of the following year, I was awaken early one Saturday morning about 5:30 A.M. Since I usually get up early every morning for either work or church I was not happy to be up that early on my only day to rest. Nevertheless, the Spirit of the Lord led me downstairs to my computer. Quite honestly, I had not even thought about the book. I didn't think about writing, or anything else for the previous three and a half months. I began to read what I had written almost one year earlier. I was amazed. The writings stated my goals, my dreams, and my objectives. It stated my desires and the calling I felt God had placed on my life. I sat there very early that Saturday morning and wrote my thoughts and feelings and what I was experiencing. All of that ultimately led to this moment. So sit back, relax, and share my story.

CHAPTER 1

THE AWAKENING

When I was six years old, I used to envision what my life would be like at the age of 30. To a little girl, 30 seemed *old*. I had my entire life mapped out because if I could achieve certain goals, I would have been productive to society, and lived a life to be envied. Now as an adult I realize that 30 is not old, but I used that birthday as an opportunity to evaluate my life.

Many of the goals that I had may sound familiar to most women. Did you ever say as a little girl, "When I get older I want to be married with two children, a boy and a girl"? "I want the boy to be older than the girl so he can take care of his little sister." While playing house, our imagination would roam down many avenues of what life would be like when we got older.

For me, I also dreamed of having a cape cod house with a white picket fence and I wanted to be the best trial attorney on the east coast well on my way to being appointed the first African American Supreme Court Judge. Imagine my disappointment when Clarence Thomas beat me to the punch. At any rate, I still had a chance to be the first African American Vice President I thought.

At the age of thirty, I realized how truly blessed I was. Married to the perfect mate, with two children together, Jesse and Emani. And yes, Jesse is older than his sister by five years. I have a beautiful cape cod house in a nice quiet community I dreamed of. The one goal that I did not accomplish is that I am not an attorney.

Life has its twists and turns, but I managed to find a career I loved so much it overrode those political desires and aspirations. I became a Certified Financial Planner and Financial Advisor as well as an entertainer and small business owner. I have had the privilege of hosting a television show for over five years and it all has been very rewarding.

As a financial planner, I shared a relationship with my clients that gave me an extended family and valuable friends. The best feeling that I get is when my clients introduce me to their friends and family as their advisor at a family outing. Very often, I get the look from the family members like "You and your advisor are friends?" Their faces have a look of utter disbelief. The funniest looks come when people look as if they recognize me but they don't know where or how. What I try to determine is whether the amazement lies with the fact that I'm black or that their family member actually has an advisor. And that is not unusual. I know many advisors that don't have a real relationship with their clients. I know who my client's attorneys and their accountants are. I know who they are looking to use when they purchase a house. Why? Because they call me to ask for a recommendation, or to talk with the person they selected. I am still overwhelmed, even to this day, when I see the look on someone's face when they realized their dream to purchase a house, they have enough money to cover their children's college needs, they can start the business they always dreamed about having, or they can retire five years earlier, if they choose.

All of this is based on a plan we devised together and reviewed periodically. Many of them are comforted with the possibility of achieving those goals. And those same family members and friends begin to look at my clients differently. It is the look that says, "How can she/he afford an advisor? Where do they stand financially? I make more than them, how come I don't have an advisor? What can I do to get my financial affairs in order?" Even with all of that, I always considered what I was doing as valuable and necessary for "the client". It was a job-a very rewarding job, but a job nonetheless. I can go one step further and say it was my career. I loved what I did for a living. Besides, it is also very lucrative.

Another goal that I had was to make over $100,000 annually by the age of thirty. But the one thing I never realized was how important it was to have a plan prior to going through an experience where you would need a plan.

CHAPTER 2

A LIFE CHANGING EVENT

On the morning of September 11th, I went to work bright and early. It was primary election day in New York City. It was a beautiful day, a clear blue sky, people hustling, scrambling off to work. I worked on the 73rd floor in the World Trade Center building Two.

Most people knew I was in my office because I was a workaholic. The state of the economy in 2001 and the fact that I was at a new firm deemed I work an average of 70 hours each week. I'd just celebrated my one- year anniversary with my new job the month before. Between the market being down and the team still trying to adjust to the new surroundings, it was amazing that any of us had a chance to go home at night to rest. We practically lived at the office. We were in the process of transferring all of our clients' assets, which was very time consuming.

In order to make sure each client is well taken care of, as a financial planner, clients must have every incentive previously had at the old firm. Those details often take a year to eighteen months. Needless to say, we all practically lived at work.

Quite frankly, because the pressure was so great, I made the decision to separate from the team and begin production as a Planner and Advisor on my own. It was always my intention to become independent. The original agreement was I would help transfer the accounts to the new firm which typically takes approximately three to six months. Afterwards, I could concentrate on developing my own book of business while still supporting the team. After the first year, I would slowly transition out of the team. After working together for eight years, my associate and I wanted the clients to get used to the idea that I would no longer be around.

However, things did not work out quite the way I intended. Because of the condition of the market I never had the opportunity to fully concentrate on my own business. Therefore I made an executive decision that no time would be the best time. At that point, I experienced major relief. By the end of the year, I would be on my own. So there wasn't any question about my whereabouts on the morning of September 11th.

As you are now aware, tragedy struck that morning as we were attacked by spineless terrorists. But unknowingly, I had come into my office and I laid my briefcase down. I was about to go and speak to one of the interns from the team because some changes were about to take place in the office. Originally, I was scheduled to leave my partnership in December of that year. However, after serious contemplation and several meetings with management, a mutual decision was made to terminate the partnership that I was in for the last eight years immediately, effective September 15th.

So, I came out of my office, and stopped at the desk to speak with an assistant. That's when Tower One was hit. Now mind you, I was located in Tower Two. We could feel the initial impact of the plane. The building began to vibrate and the lights flickered off and on. There was a lot of movement. I think that might have lasted a full thirty seconds but it felt like two or three minutes. I couldn't see anything based on where my office was located, so I did not panic immediately.

As a matter of fact, my two assistants were like "Let's go, let's go, let's go." But at the time, I didn't think that was necessary. Of course my thoughts were, as an advisor you need to be at your desk to make money. If you're not at your desk evaluating or researching a stock, speaking to a client, or placing orders, you were out trying to attract new clients. Therefore it would have been counterproductive for me to be away from my desk. There is no way you can make money away from your desk. And certainly, that is our ultimate objective, to make money for our clients. Not to mention properly servicing our clients helps us to make money for ourselves.

Then, I walked across the hall to my partner's office and saw the burning papers twirling outside the window. It looked like the New York Yankees were celebrating winning the World Series with a ticker tape parade. As I looked out the window in disbelief, the Spirit of the Lord spoke to me and told me to go. I did not hesitate. I moved quickly. I went into my office, grabbed my briefcase and told my assistants, "Let's go!" Although, they suggested the same thought not even one minute earlier.

On our way to the staircase on the 73rd floor, we passed the receptionist desk. Our receptionist grabbed her purse and began to walk down the stairs with us. Apparently, we were probably one of the first ones to leave the floor. From what I gathered after the fact, several male associates made sure almost everyone left the floor.

Many of my colleagues caught the elevator and then walked down from the 44th fl. As we began to walk down from the 73rd floor, announcements were being made over the Public Announcement system, "Building Two is secure. Building Two is secure. You can go back to your office. Building Two is secure. You are safe. You can choose to leave the building, but I assure you Building Two is secure." This announcement was made over and over again. As a matter of fact, I found comfort in the announcement.

Meanwhile, while we were walking down the steps, word began to spread through the stairway the building had been hit by an airplane. I thought it was an accident. A small CNN plane had lost control and hit the Tower, nothing major. It was just a small accident. Someone opened the door to the 53rd floor stairway and I decided to take the elevator down to the 44th floor so I could return to my office. At that point, somehow my assistants and I were temporarily separated. Getting on the elevator was probably one of the stupidest decisions that I have ever made in my life. But I took the elevator from the 53rd floor to the 44th floor.

Let me explain something about the 44th floor. If you've ever been in the World Trade Center, then you know that the 44th floor is where you can take different elevators to different floors. So for me to go back to 73, I had to go through the 44th floor. When I got on the 44th floor, I glanced at the TV monitors confirming the story I heard on the staircase regarding the plane. What was still not yet confirmed was that it was a CNN plane and that it was an accident. Both which we now know, were not true. I had made the decision to go back upstairs. I reconnected with my assistants and walked over to the elevators. I thank God because I hesitated. That hesitation saved my life.

Once again, I felt the Spirit of the Lord upon me telling me to wait. That hesitation caused me not to get on the elevator. That's when Tower Two was hit-the building that I was in-the building that was secure. The plane went right through the floors that I was on my way to. Immediately I knew we were being attacked. People died on the elevators that I had just come off of. Elevator chutes popped, causing explosions and fireballs to shoot out. People standing outside of the elevator doors were severely burned. I was standing in front of an elevator door and it did not open. The first thing I did was drop to my knees and began to pray. I said, "Father, please forgive me." If I did not survive, if I did not make it out of that building, I would be in heaven today without a shadow of doubt. After that, I began to pray, "God cover me, God cover the people I'm with. Let us get out of here safely." My assistant asked me later that day how did I have the mind, attitude, and strength to pray at that precise moment. I said to her that I had no choice but to pray. What else would I do? If we were to have any chance of surviving, it would have to be God's will. I had to let my requests be known unto the Lord. I wanted to survive.

At the same time, bodies were flying because of the impact of the plane. The building was shaking, glass shattered everywhere, and smoke began to infiltrate the 44th floor. After what seemed like fifty years, but probably was closer to four or five minutes, a dead calm began to gulf the air. The chaos just died down, almost instantly. I did not stick around. The Lord spoke to me again, and I walked to a stairway that I did not even know existed.

It's funny how we can work in an environment and not commit to our memories, our surroundings. I never realized how important it is to observe your exit points everywhere you go. I began to walk down the stairway and there was an eerie calm. Usually, when faced with a potentially dangerous situation, there is chaos and confusion. People tend to panic, stampedes can occur. But on that day, that did not happen. As a matter of fact, I thought it was very ironic that the stairway was not crowded. There were floors where it was almost empty. As I was walking down, there was no smoke and the area was well lit.

On the 44th floor though, it was apparent something serious had occurred. You could really see the effects of the tragedy. Literally, on the stairs, there was not activity. If I had not been in the building, I would have thought I imagined the whole situation. I began to question the severity of the incident. I was convincing myself that it was not as significant as our being attacked. Although I knew in my spirit that was what had happened.

There was a young lady that we connected with on the staircase who was asthmatic. Walking down the stairs was beginning to affect her breathing seriously. My assistants and I decided that we were all going to get out of the building together. So I said to her, "We're not going to leave you. So if you need to stay here, I'll stand with you. I know I'm getting out of the building safely but, I prefer not to stop. So if you must have an attack, I'd appreciate it if you could wait until we got to Broadway." Needless to say, she did get out of the building with us.

I did not realize the devastation that had occurred until I hit the mezzanine. If you know anything about The World Trade Center, it was known for its glass panes. The glass planes stemmed from the ground to the ceiling. The revolving doors were made of glass; glass was everywhere. The mezzanine was once a beautiful place to visit and just gaze outside. Many pictures have been taken on the mezzanine of the World Trade Center. When I hit the mezzanine, my first thought was "FREEDOM!" Those glass doors represented an escape for me. Go through the revolving doors, and run! I would have been running for my dear life. I could get out of a situation that could be potentially dangerous, hazardous to my health. It might kill me.

Although I felt comfort on the stairway, I still knew we were under attack and while walking down the stairs, the news that the Pentagon had been hit and another plane crashed in Pennsylvania spread and that news laid heavy on my heart. As far as I was concerned, another plane could be on the way. I knew we were still in trouble. The greatest fear I had the entire day came at that point. There were firemen and police officers telling me that I could not exit out of those doors-the very doors that led to freedom for me. They were keeping me captive.

Little did I know, debris was falling everywhere and it was to my advantage not to go that route. I thank God for the professionals. The Policemen and Firemen represented true heroism on September 11th. But the hardest thing that I had to do on that day was to walk further into the World Trade Center. I had to go downstairs to the floor where all of the stores were. I walked passed the Diamond Hut, Strawberries, the N&R train, the Watch Store, The Disney Store, Nine West, all of the stores that I visited almost weekly. Every so often, medics and authorities would pass the crowd of people attempting to get out of the building with an injured man or woman. I saw people bleeding profusely, limbs cut off, shocked people experiencing asthma attacks, people who probably never had heart conditions experiencing pains in the chest. I saw everything you would not wish on your worst enemy. Ironically, in hindsight, the vision of the movie "Dead Man Walking" can effectively describe how I felt. The point when the convict about to be executed had to walk the long walkway to his death. It was at that moment I felt most vulnerable. I was full of despair, lacking hope to know life as I knew it would never be the same. If I ever thought that I was going to die, it was then, walking down that long, long corridor.

But as quickly as the thought came, I rebuked it. I was going to get out of that building. A friend later said while comforting one of my sisters before hearing from me, "Nicole is going to get out of the building even if she has to shimmey down the wall. Now you know your sister." It was actually comic relief in a tough situation.

After going up the escalator, finally, I was out of the building. I exited for the last time, Building 5 right next to the infamous Krispy Kreme Doughnut Shop. I did not turn around. I just kept walking. I walked and thanked God, but I did not look back. I felt like I had the same instructions Lot and his wife had in the Bible. If you turn around, you will surely die.

When I reached Broadway, I finally turned around. I looked at an airplane sitting in the building I had just come out of. It was like a picture and did not seem real. There I was standing on Broadway Avenue looking at the World Trade Center standing with an airplane in it. I have no recollection of how Building One looked. What happened to the first plane? What I remember is the sky was clear, a perfect blue with little or no clouds in sight. An airplane's wings were hanging out the building. The flames were a perfect burnt orange and the clouds of smoke swirled perfectly in the air. The picture was worthy of painting had the experience not been a reality. What I never expected to see was bodies falling out the sky, people attempting to jump from a skyscraper. Tears began to stream down my face. I had not cried the entire time beforehand. I was trying to be strong for my assistants who were traumatized at that moment. But that was the last straw and I think everyone there cried at one point or another. I have visions and dreams to this day. I have seen things I will never forget, certain things that will haunt me for the rest of my life. There are things that keep me from sleeping more often than not. I thank God he saw fit to save me. At that moment I realized I was not far enough away. Call it instinct. Call it God watching over me, whatever. All I knew was that we had to get away from there.

At that time we were all trying to call loved ones to let them know we were still alive. I managed to get through to my sister's job in New York City but she did not go to work on that day. This was prior to the buildings collapsing. My sister was still in New Jersey trying to enroll my niece into a new school. So my family had to wait hours before hearing from me. I made the decision to walk over to Battery Park City.

At that moment I was a little worried about my associate. She decided to go and vote before coming to work. Therefore, based on her anticipated arrival in the office, I half expected her to be near or even in the building. Either way, I always had complete access to her home so at least I would be able to use the phone to try and reach my family.

The four of us began to walk, proceeding down the block toward Fulton Street. We moved on to Wall Street and then to Battery Park. We circled around the FDR Drive. But before we crossed the street to continue on our way to Battery Park City, we stood near the overpass just gazing up at the sky. From that vantage point we were able to see things we should have never looked for. You could see the tail of the plane hanging out. So instantly I knew that is where the plane initially hit. I felt so close. Somehow I could see people, people that I knew were destined to die that day. I knew it was impossible for them to exit the building.

When we finally arrived at Battery Park City on Rector Street we found my associate alive and very happy to see us. The first thing we did was hug and cry together. The five of us stood praying, crying, meditating, and thanking God for deliverance. As soon as we got there, Building Two, the building I used to work in, the building I had just come out of, the building I must have left at least seven pairs of shoes at, collapsed. It just fell.

I never, never imagined, even in my wildest dreams, it was even a possibility, but I was safe. Safe from the bricks, the falling debris, the broken glass, everything. The only thing that traveled my way was the dust particles. Rector Street was a blanket of dust. Dust was in the air, traveling in the windows into people's houses and into my lungs. When the building fell, it became as dark as a pitch-black sky in the heart of the country. The smoke was so thick the sky that once was blue, turned midnight for at least thirty minutes. I don't know the actual time between Building Two and Building One falling, but I do know that the skies had just begun to clear from the collapse of Building Two when Building One put us back into the pitch-dark nighttime atmosphere. My heart fell with the fall of the two buildings. A piece of my soul died on that day. It took us about an additional two hours to communicate with our families to let them know that we were alive.

Shortly after the second Tower collapsed, the electricity failed in the building we were in. No lights, no TV, no radio, nothing. The only thing that was still working was the telephone and to this very day, I'm still not certain how that was even possible. Even my associate's laptop gave way after a while. When we first arrived at the house, it was still up and running. We began to email family and friends. That was nothing but the grace of God.

I finally had a chance to speak with my family a little after 12:00 P.M. The first person I spoke with was my mom. I could not reach my husband and I knew he was worried sick about me. My husband Jesse was home getting ready for work. He is a TV producer and director that very often freelance with outside cable companies. After getting dressed, he got into the car and began to drive. He turned on the radio and heard the radio personality telling everyone to stay calm, don't panic. Instantly he thought another artist had passed away. As he was driving, the news that one of the Twin Towers had been hit, smacked him in the face making him lose his breath. He didn't even make it off the block.

Immediately, he drove the car in reverse down the block back to the house. The funny thing is that as he got out of the car, he looked across the street and noticed several middle-eastern men cutting a tree down in front of one of the neighbor's yards. He walked into the house leaving the front door wide open. A next-door neighbor came to the house to make sure Jesse was holding up well. Jesse was attempting to convince himself that I was in the building that was not hit. That was until the second building was hit. Then he was trying to convince himself that I was in the first building that was hit. Why, because based on where the buildings were hit, I still had a chance to survive had I been in building one.

By that time, several neighbors had gathered at my house. They were all watching TV in my living room hoping for the best when Tower Two collapsed. Jesse sat in utter disbelief, still trying to convince himself I was alive. But shortly after Tower Two fell, Tower One came down too. That was it. I was dead- any chance of my being alive was crushed with the buildings. Jesse said that he began to think; what did I wear to work that day, what did I smell like, did he tell me that he loved me. He said he forgot he had children and had it not been for the neighbors reminding him about the children, he would not have remembered them. He did go to the school to pick up my son Jesse who had overheard the teachers talking about the Towers collapsing.

So by the time my husband went to the school, my son was dealing with the fact that his mother was dead. My son saw his dad coming into the school building from his classroom and felt it was confirmation for him. They both went to pick up my daughter Emani. Emani was five years old and enjoying the first grade. My husband made the decision to let her stay in school since she did not know what was going on. It was the best thing he could have done. She did not have to suffer with the thought of her mommy not coming home ever again. It was bad enough that Lil' Jesse had to deal with that trauma.

Interestingly enough, he deals with it even today. If I'm leaving the house, he questions me as if he is my Dad-Mom, "Where are you going, how long will you be there, when will you be back." I have to keep telling him, I'm the mother, and you're the child. I'll be okay. Fortunately enough, my husband and my son heard from me by about 1:00 that afternoon. They did not have to wait eight to ten hours like some of the horror stories of the other victims.

Shortly after we were all able to reach our loved ones, early in the afternoon, security in Battery Park City began to cry loudly on each floor. They were knocking on everyone's door. The building was being evacuated. Our experience was hardly over. As we made our way from the second floor to the outside, relying upon feeling the walls and flashlights in the darkness, I began to wonder where was I going. How was I going to get home?

I walked out of Battery Park City and immediately knew what my true purpose in life was. Why? Security was directing all residents of Battery Park City to the water to get on boats to either Jersey City or Staten Island. Yes, boats. They had both cargo and freight boats available for evacuation. Understand… there were provisions in place to take the wealthy to safety. I realized at that moment the wealthy had plans in place to handle unforeseen circumstances, unforeseen incidents. We don't have a plan and I realized then how seriously we needed to get one.

Now the people in Battery Park City do not look like you and me. I have friends, associates, and colleagues, who did not get home until after 12:00 that night, if they were lucky, and many of them did not get home until the following day. I was fortunate enough to get home by 4:00 that afternoon because I was at the right place at the right time benefiting from the provisions the wealthy set up for themselves. It was not by accident I was there. I began to think, as I got on the boat, a large, cargo boat, that I was safe. Finally, that part of my life, that tragedy was almost over. But no, that would have been too easy. I truly believe that God has a sense of humor, even when I feel certain things aren't funny.

While on a boat going to Jersey City, NJ, my hometown, where I grew up, announcements were being made the boat was too large to dock at the port and we would have to change boats in the middle of the water. So now I have a vision of surviving the World Trade Center attack only to fall off the boat while transferring onto another boat in the middle of the water and not surviving. I began to laugh hysterically, while tears streamed down my face. I was a complete basket case. Any control I had was gone at that moment. Since I did not have my shoes, my socks were completely damaged in the process.

But again, I survived. I get down to Jersey City and I immediately look to go home. My assistants, my associate and I stayed together until we all arrived in Jersey City. Then each of us went our separate ways. My associate who lived in Battery Park City went home with me to meet up with a friend from my house. I lived approximately forty-five minutes away from Jersey City. But I could have gone to mom's house or even my mother in law.

However, I was determined to get home, to my house with my family. I managed to meet my mother in law and God showed favor on her. The city of Jersey City was completely shut down but the police officers allowed her to break through the barriers to pick me up. Traffic was being directed away from downtown Jersey City and she was the only one given permission to drive toward that direction.

I also have a friend who received a phone call from her sister because her sister saw me when I got off the boat. My friend Denise said that her sister told her that I was alive, I was okay, and I looked a mess. And I really did. By that time I didn't have on a jacket or shoes, and I was completely covered with dust from head to toe. That day my hair was truly gray. Denise knew I was in the building. The instant she heard about the Tower getting hit, she called everyone in the church and said "Nicole is in the building, start praying. Pray that God protects and delivers her." Everyone in my church was praying for my safety. After Denise spoke to her sister, she gathered up some clothes, shoes, and food and came Downtown dragging her daughter, Bianca. I'm sure Bianca had no idea what in the world was going on. She probably thought her mother was crazy. I don't know exactly where she was going but Denise managed to convince the authorities she needed to get to Exchange Place to pick me up. I never saw Denise but she made it all of the way to the water down by the Harbor. I didn't even know she was down there. I only concentrated on trying to get home.

Finally, I arrived home around 4:00 p.m. and I completely embrace my family. Once my associate was gone, I began to watch television. I sat in my living room for six or seven days in front of the television watching the death toll continue to rise. I watched what happened in Pennsylvania, in Washington, and in New York, over and over again. I did not leave my seat. I did not sleep. The only time I left the house was to go to the hospital because I could not breathe and to my mother's house so she could be firmly convinced I was alive and in the flesh. I couldn't even stay at the hospital. I didn't feel safe. I really thought the hospital might be attacked. So against the doctor's advice, I checked out. What did I do? I got back on my couch and continued to torture myself. The death toll kept going up and up and I just kept thanking God over and over again. I scared my husband so much because quite unexpectedly I would fall to my knees and begin to pray.

I thank God for Jesse because after he heard my entire ordeal, he troubleshot the phones and carried my burden for me. He spoke to everyone who called, explained the situation and the state I was in. He would not allow anyone to talk to me, completely complying with my wishes. Now that I think about it, he went through a major trauma as well. To take on my feelings and forget about him self, bearing the pain and agony he went through thinking I was dead was beyond fortunate. I was and am honored to be in relationship with such an awesome man.

At some point, on the forth or fifth day, I began to think. What if? What would have happened if I did not survive? What if I were permanently disabled? Many people lost arms, legs, and other parts of their bodies. Others were severely burned. As a matter of fact, you didn't have to be involved in the tragedy of the World Trade Center to experience disability. Some people might be more likely to experience disability than to die prematurely. If you're injured and you can't go to work, drawing a disability salary, could you maintain your lifestyle you built up for yourself? I began to think about all the people who lost their jobs. What if? Where would my family be? What was the state of my household? Did I have a plan in place? I began to evaluate these very same questions I generally ask my clients as a result of my personal tragedy.

CHAPTER 3

DO YOU HAVE A PLAN?

At that point in my life being a Financial Planner took on an entirely different meaning. I lived through an ordeal myself. Being a mother of two small children, married and blessed with a home in a nice community made me realize how vulnerable I could possibly be. My home was not completely paid for yet. My husband and I largely rely on each other's income to maintain our standard of living. We are probably classified as a middle class income household. Jesse and I have desires and dreams for each of our children. If they choose to go to Harvard, we want to be capable of making that dream come.

If I had not survived, would my husband have had to worry about how the bills were going to be paid the next month? Or better yet, would he possibly lose the house because he could no longer afford it? Would my family have to suffer emotionally with losing a wife and mother and then move back into the very projects we worked hard to move out of? Did I have insurance in place? Did I have emergency cash set aside?

After contemplating the things most important to me, I came to the conclusion working seventy hours a week was no longer acceptable. I wanted to be around to see my children grow up. Financially, that is not a decision one can make overnight. I decided to figure out, even if I could not afford it at that precise moment, how I would change my plans to open that opportunity in the near future. I realized the importance of putting my plan in place prior to needing one. That's where many of us end up in an awkward position.

Before beginning the process of implementing a plan, you have the chance to evaluate your relationship with your children, your grandchildren, and your significant other. What type of impact do you want to have on their lives? You can maintain a particular lifestyle when you're alive, when you're capable of working, but what about when you can't. I thank God I had a plan. When devising a plan, you can evaluate what's important to you individually and begin to work towards those goals.

Through that evaluation process, you can make the decision whether or not you need a new job, additional schooling, or should you just step out on faith and start that business you have been dreaming about for years. Are you one of those people that keep a detailed plan of how to carry out your dreams that sit in a notebook you carry everywhere you go? Every time you talk to your friends, are you're telling them something new about how you would make your dreams come true? When is the time to act on those plans?

Through my entire ordeal, the one thing my husband said was he never thought about our financial state God forbid had I not survived. He was reassured we had a plan in place. That has always been the security I would want should I ever have to face a life-threatening situation. I relied upon our plan also as I made the decision not return to work immediately after the tragedy. There were several reasons for my decision.

First, my firm had relocated our office to the Madison Square Garden. The first day that everyone went to the office, there was a bomb scare at the Madison Square Garden. My colleagues had to walk down 34 flights of stairs. Any thoughts that I had about going back to New York left before they hit the first floor. I figured that I was an educated woman with an excellent work track record. If my company could not find space available for me in New Jersey, then I would be forced to look at other options.

From a business perspective, since I had to start from scratch again, it would benefit me to start in a place I was familiar with and where people where familiar with me. Because my husband and I owned a television production company that was known for creating original programming, I've had the opportunity to host a television show for several years. That platform assisted me in creating relationships with various community leaders, which ultimately led my company to get involved locally through a community association. Being active in the community and being on television everyday worked to my advantage.

At any rate, for the first time since giving birth to my son, my paycheck would be similar to the income I was making in high school. It was like starting all over but I knew all the sacrifices would be worth it?

In the times we now live in, I am not the only one that sees the need to determine what sacrifices we might and should make to benefit our loved ones in the future. The question for many is where do you start?

CHAPTER 4

PREPARING YOUR FAMILY

FOR EMERGENCIES

Having money set aside for emergencies would probably be the most immediate need for many families today. If I didn't have such a plan in place I wouldn't have had the peace of mind to pursue my deepest endeavors. Upon my decision to leave work, emergency cash money subsidized my family income replacing what I originally contributed to the household. But, it was not at all easy.

Many days I would question my husband to make sure I had the support I needed to redevelop a new business in order to educate my community and develop a new clientele. I also decided to take a hiatus from the family television business as well. I knew building a new business would be difficult and time consuming. I didn't want to be an unnecessary financial burden to him. I was already an emotional basket case trying to step out on faith but my husband was totally supportive. He could have told me to get a new job. Instead of building a business I could have been waiting tables. Besides having an emergency plan in place it also helped to have a support system during the transition. My husband's support gave me the opportunity to develop my business the way that would ultimately benefit my clients the most effectively. Now I was in a position to get started evaluating the needs of my clients. Not everyone has the encouragement and support I had to develop financial strategies and plans for the future.

Again from my experience I was able to assess the circumstances and needs of the people I wanted to serve. I understood I would need to make it mandatory for my clients to complete a financial plan before seriously discussing investment strategies. This is the best way to see what needs and issues exist. There are exceptions to every rule. Not all clients see the need to do this, especially those primarily interesting in seeking only investment strategies. Still, I inform them about the importance of having a plan and strongly suggest they consider putting one in place if they don't already have one.

Most of us see the importance of maintaining a plan for emergencies but few of us see the urgency of setting the plan up immediately. Some think it sounds good and it's something they will eventually get around to. Your emergency could come next week! People have been losing their jobs left and right.

As the state of the economy continues to be extremely fragile, especially since the peak in the market in March of 2000, many corporations are being forced to undergo major layoffs to reduce company expenses. This occurred even prior to September 11th. I'm sure you know someone who has been laid off, offered an early Retirement package, or a severance package.

For African Americans in particular, it's the world's greatest gift. Very often you could be entitled to a severance package determined by the years of service to the company. But not so fast…immediately Uncle Sam is entitled to his share. So maybe you will get two thirds of what you originally anticipated. Now, do you create a budget with the thought in mind that jobs are scarce and you might need to analyze your financial future? Or, do you run and buy that car you have been dreaming about? What about the new living room set, or the washing machine? I got it. You've been working since you graduated high school and you need a vacation. Finally, you have the resources to go on your dream vacation. Just a thought, but you might need that severance money in a few months when you're still unemployed.

If we budget ourselves accordingly, this scenario could apply to you. It's so amazing how we can save $100 per month for a whole year towards a vacation but we can't save $100 a month for emergencies. Imagine if you received that same severance package and you saved three months emergency cash? In addition, once the severance assets are depleted you will collect unemployment. That plan just gave you six months to look for a new employer. How? Rather than running out and spending the money as soon as you got it, by setting some aside for bills your lifestyle will not be affected.

How many times have you had extra money but chose not to think ahead about future bills and paid the price later? Suffering a disability or loss of job can be devastating when you don't have an emergency plan in place for such unexpected situations. Some people have even lost their homes to foreclosure because of the lack of proper planning and saving money. Do you want to be in a position like that?

When I make statements like that, I always hear people say, "I can't afford to save money. It's just not possible." People even say what I promote is unrealistic in urban communities.

Unfortunately, the reality is most African Americans *are* living from paycheck to paycheck. And if they aren't, then they are approximately two months away from being evicted.

But let's look at how we spend money. I find it amazing that women can't set aside money for emergencies but they don't miss a hair appointment every week. An average doobie costs at least $10. That's forty dollars a month. We get our nails done twice a month and if we throw in a pedicure, we just spent another fifty dollars. A design and tip refills add another thirty dollars a month. We work hard all week and each of us needs a break so girl's night out once a month is mandatory. I'll give you that you're getting into the party for free. But even the best looking ladies must pay for the first drink not to look like she is waiting for a man to pay for her enjoyment. The outfit you purchased for the happening party cost approximately $65 dollars and you bought that on sale.

For all of you that attend church on Sunday morning, there are certain churches that a new outfit each month is a must.

Now church is a totally different expense. Why? You've got to look good for God. An entire ensemble just might run you approximately $100. And if you throw in the hat, you've just spent another $30. Just look at the choices you make.

Finally, for everyone that can't save and you work everyday, do you bring your lunch to work? If the answer is no, you're probably spending at least $7 for lunch. Normally, you pick up coffee and a bagel for $1.00 and if you're anything like me, at about 3:00 each day, you must have that soda and a snack running you an additional $1.50. That's about $9.50 a day give or take a dollar or two. By the end of the week you spend $50 dollars and each month that's almost $200.

Now I'm not just picking on the women, men have their devices as well. Some men spend so much money on maintenance of their automobiles. A bottle of Armor All, Fresh Scent, and Turtle Wax totals about $15. The instant you get a spot on your white on white Air Force One's, it's time for a new pair. Cleaning them is not an option. That costs about $100 given the size of your foot. Now, the clubs that the ladies get in for free…cost you $20. Men generally hit the clubs at least twice a month. That's $40. Buying drinks as soon as you get it, especially if it is a classy joint will cost you. Instead of spending $50 to $100 you'll spend $150 before you even blinked. That's because you've got to have Henessy or other top shelf liqueurs. Your clothes are so expensive and unfortunately, you don't have any stores like the ladies' $10 spot. Each outfit runs you at least $150 if you want to attract wifey. If not, $100 will do if you don't want to be the laughing stock of the party. Men must look like they are rolling in dough. But just to drive the point home, the average man is driving around in a car that he can't really afford. If your car note is over $500 and you are living in subsidized housing with your girl, that right there needs analyzing.

This doesn't apply everyone, mostly just the people who say they can't save. Evaluate the choices you make. I do have clients who really can't afford to save money. But even they can save for retirement. We must remember each of us will encounter a situation where the need for emergency cash will arise.

For example, while I was still rebuilding my business, my husband, my daughter, and I were in a car accident, which totaled my car. Now, living in the suburbs means you must have transportation. We needed to buy another vehicle right away. Emergency cash set aside made that possible.

During the winter, hot water heaters tend to burst. If that were to happen to you, must you sacrifice the mortgage payment to fix the heater or to get a new one? Now that's an emergency. That is what the money should be for.

Entertainers too are not exempt from the need to save either. Why do many entertainers file for bankruptcy? Here's my opinion. I look at the lifestyle of entertainers, particularly music artists. Very often, people get caught up in the glamour of success. Because an artist has a hit record on the charts, people perceive that the entertainer is financially secure. After all, they have attained a level of success. Or did they?

Therefore the artist feels the pressure to maintain a particular image. If Bentleys are the new wave or Cadillac Escalades, how dare they have a Ford Explorer? If everyone is purchasing million dollar homes, having a condo is not good enough. The clothes you wear must have a name brand on it and the diamonds must be carets. However, most people at the beginning of their careers cannot even afford these things. They become indebted or obligated to the record company and therefore their money is used to pay off major expenses accumulated at the beginning stages of their careers.

The first thing entertainers *should* do is put themselves on a budget. Most artists cannot guarantee what their income will be in eighteen months. What is hot today might not be next month. With a budget in place, the likelihood of losing assets through default is minimized. I recommend entertainers set aside six months living expenses. Then there is that much time to make additional money. Now, if they should want to purchase a house or a fancy car, they would be better positioned to make that decision. Too often artists do not properly manage their money or balance their checkbook. They just continue to spend. When the financial drought comes, the artist is left feeling the pinch of not having money. Diamond rings on your fingers cannot pay the mortgage bills. But that six-month emergency cash stash, just might help you out. It's better than not having anything.

One of my closest friends is an entertainer who has been an artist for over twenty years. This gentleman was a pioneer in the Rap industry. I talked to him about what did with the money he earned as an artist. Without realizing it, the young man invested a little of his money each time he received royalties and significant dollars in real estate and a savings account. He did not want to worry about paying bills. The property he purchased was income-producing property. After a while, his royalty checks stopped coming in. But by that time, he had already replaced his royalties with income producing investments. His emergency cash money was also in tact. Years later, he was mindful of how he benefited from setting aside cash. Had he not set aside those dollars, where would he be after his income completely dried up?

Another emergency that often occurs are unexpected deaths in the family. Must the entire family depend on the one family member who had a plan to handle the financial obligations of a funeral? Or do you wait for the sympathy envelopes filled with financial gifts to start flowing in before you can determine what type of procession you can have? What if the services are out of state? Can you just jump on a plane and not worry that hotel accommodations are going to devastate you financially? Or must you phone ahead to see if you can stay with Aunt Mae? Emergencies!

CHAPTER 5

OBTAINING LIFE INSURANCE

I mentioned that my husband was not concerned about his financial future if I had not survived because we had insurance plans in place. But let me tell you what happened to us. I always told my husband, "Baby, God forbid something should ever happen to me, call Eileen. All of my important papers are in my office in our file." He remembered that. But when the Towers collapsed, all of my important papers collapsed with them. Now, no one could ever predict that. It made me think.

People usually don't know pertinent information if something were to happen to their mates, particularly women.

My husband knew exactly where to go to determine where he stood financially. After the tragedy though, he wanted to know more details about our insurance. What type of insurance plans did we have, how much, who are the carriers? Did I set up settlement options? What did he need in order to contact the companies? I found these to be very important questions all of us should ask. My husband no longer took it for granted someone else would handle the affairs for him.

But even in my preparing additional information for him, I realized that I set up one of our insurance policies to automatically withdraw the premiums out of our checking account quarterly. About six months after the tragedy, I noticed a payment being withdrawn out of the checking account that looked totally unfamiliar. After inquiring about the withdrawal, I realized I had even more insurance than I originally thought.

Now, if I'm the planner and I didn't know about the additional insurance, without records how would my husband know what to look for? The obvious lesson for me was to have important documents and information in a place easily accessible to the people who will ultimately need it.

So many of us go without obtaining insurance thinking there will be time for that when we get around to it. Recently, I spoke with a young lady who is in the process of applying for life insurance. She is a small business owner and a single parent with two boys and a girl. At the tender age of 28, she experienced three deaths of people close to her in one year alone. That was the primary reason why she inquired about insurance.

Being an entrepreneur has its advantages, but one of the disadvantages is the owner is responsible for everything. No one is there to make sure you have life insurance, health insurance, or even a retirement plan in place. The owner must also manage their books. Despite the condition of the economy, the bills must still get paid. Many small businesses have been suffering as a result. Therefore, what once was a priority such as insurance, takes a back seat to what's actually in the business owners face to keep the business afloat. This young lady ultimately decided it was not the time to purchase the insurance.

However, it was important for me to show her delicately how vulnerable her children would be if she were in an accident or suffered from a premature death or disability. Normally, delaying the process several months, may not be a major issue if she worked in corporate America. Most companies offer at least a minimal insurance policy and health insurance. But in her situation, her need for insurance was an ultimate priority, especially since premature death was an uncertain possibility and she had three children. What if one of the children suffered a health condition that required medical attention? One child could break an arm or leg and cripple her financially.

While she was thinking about finances, I was thinking about the well being of her three children she loved dearly and did everything she could to provide for. I knew she needed someone to advise her and remind her of what she originally stated as a priority. She worked hard to provide a better life and opportunity for her children. She was concentrating so much on the present she needed me to show her how to consider the future as well to make sure her children had the life she wanted so much for them. I knew she would want them to have those opportunities even if she could not be there to share them for some reason. It is easy to overlook these things when we are just trying to get by today.

Sometimes we think once we have the insurance though that we are taken care of. We might get the insurance through our job or take the initiative to get it on our own. When we purchase the insurance, we think long and hard about the people we want to have the money should something happen to us. That might be our spouse, our parents, or our children. What we don't do is evaluate our policies periodically to see if our circumstances are the same.

Well, what do I mean? Divorce is both popular and something we choose not to discuss with other people. It makes the individual feel as a failure. But in not communicating about divorce, we often forget to handle key financial issues relating to the relationship, namely changing the beneficiary on the insurance policy. Very often, I have clients who are on their second marriage. They come to me with their new husband or wife to complete a financial plan. As I begin to review the insurance policies, I find that the ex-spouse stands to benefit financially if the client were to die. When the divorce took place, the client never bothered to change the beneficiary on their insurance policies, especially the policies through their employers.

Fortunately, I am able to change my client's situations, but how many people perish without having that opportunity? Bigger than that, what if you were the surviving spouse? You know your mate has a policy on the job so you go to collect from the employer and they tell you, "Sorry, you're not the beneficiary and I am not at liberty to disclose the information to you."

Now, the ex-spouse, who you can't stand, is driving around in a brand new car and a new wardrobe thinking, "I knew he/she still loved me." If your mate wasn't dead, at that precise moment, you could kill him or her yourself. The sad thing about this situation is, unfortunately, it occurs more often than not. How can it be prevented? If you take the time to develop a plan, you must periodically update that plan. This is particularly important when experiencing a life- changing event such as marriage, divorce, death, or the birth of a child.

Another important issue to consider is whether to leave insurance proceeds to minor children. If you are purchasing insurance to replace the potential loss of income to the household then the answer is no. If your children are left as the beneficiaries, the money will be held until your children become of age. So, how will this benefit the children when they can't even get to the money? Often that is an error we make.

As a professional, when I help a client determine what insurance needs exist, they often respond their desire is to have enough insurance to replace the income they are currently contributing to the household. They also tend to want to make sure their children's college needs are met, and possibly to pay off the mortgage of the home. However, when leaving money to minor children, the children do not have access to the money until they turn 18, possibly 21 based on which state the child resides in. Therefore, the money cannot replace what you once provided for them.

For this reason should death occur the person responsible for the children should be *considered* to have control of these funds as needed. In some cases people can be hesitant about leaving money to guardians and other family members. But what if the parties now responsible for your children were less financially secure than you, what type of environment will your children grow up in? Furthermore, you cannot control your child's life from the grave. We'd like to think our children are all college bound and willing to do everything mommy and daddy want them to do.

Throughout the years in the business however, I have seen many children turn 18, liquidate their assets that their parents designated for college, and travel the world in a brand new car. So, let's just think about this for a second. If you were 18 years old and someone told you there was $250,000 just waiting for you, what would be the first thing you would do? Now, do you really want to give your children that option? The decision of who should receive the insurance proceeds is a personal one, but when dealing with minor children, my advice is, if someone is good enough for the children, then they are good enough for the money. Besides, they need the money to raise your children in a similar lifestyle as you would. After all, that's why you chose that person in the first place…you trusted them.

Finally, securing insurance through your job does not end all responsibility. There are still other things to consider. Will it be enough to cover your insurance needs? Do you anticipate being at your job forever? Also, is the insurance policy available to you after you leave or retire?

Recently a client made the decision to retire. Her particular company allowed its employees the option to keep their insurance policy for life. Therefore it may serve to this client's particular advantage to keep her policy. She will always be insured, even when she turns ninety. There are always options to consider and it is important to be aware of all of them.

Granted with so many types of life insurance, the process can be a little intimidating when people finally do attempt to purchase coverage. Where do you even start? How do you determine what type of insurance you need? Let me first say, everyone's circumstance varies.

There are two types of polices including term insurance and a cash value policy. Term insurance covers you for a stated period of time. They have minimal cash value prior to the death of the insured because the premium charged, which increases as the risk of death increases, simply buys pure insurance. Once that time elapses, you are no longer covered. I like to compare it to auto insurance. Hopefully, you will never need it, but just in case, it's there. Many people invest in term insurance when they purchase a new home or have small children to cover major financial obligations. You pay a small premium in exchange for a large benefit. It is also the least expensive coverage available for the maximum return.

A cash value policy accumulates an economic value because the insurer charges a stated premium that is considerably higher than mortality costs require during the earlier years. Part of this overpayment accumulates as a cash surrender value. The cash surrender value can be used in two ways; the owner can surrender the policy and receive the money in cash before death or the owner can borrow against the policy. The benefit of having permanent insurance is that once the policy is purchased, your health no longer becomes an issue. Provided you maintain the terms of the policy, you will always be insured.

I know many people who make the decision to buy term insurance and invest the difference in the stock market to offset the potential need for insurance during the latter years. Once again, that becomes an individual decision that an advisor and you could make together. However, I implore you if that is a strategy you want to implement, please make sure your investment commitment is consistent. If you make the commitment to invest in a mutual fund account instead of getting permanent insurance or to save money each month do not assume you can get insurance tomorrow. I've seen several examples of people who are no longer insurable even at the age of 45. Trust me, you don't want to be in that position.

CHAPTER 6

HOW TO GIVE YOURSELF A

BREAK FROM TAXES

I want to take this time out to say thank you. Thank you to all of people fortunate enough to make it into middle class America. Thank you to all of you single people with no dependants. The economy is managed off the sweat of your labor. Your tax liability is so great and you can't even take advantage of the tax incentives set aside for you because you don't know what they are. I believe Uncle Sam is entitled to his share of money, but not a penny more. And if you don't know what tax incentives work to your advantage, or you're not astute enough to seek the expertise of a Certified Public Accountant, then I appreciate your willingness to contribute your hard earned dollars to support the land of opportunity. But just for the record, the wealthy do not pay taxes. If they do, it's very minimal. Whenever tax laws change, the wealthy hire experts to figure out the loopholes that will allow them to keep the money they make. Quick lesson, it's not what you earn but what you keep.

I know a single woman who works everyday, makes over $100,000 annually and does not have any dependents. She does not own a home and she does not have a business. She doesn't have a portfolio or any emergency cash. She doesn't have any habits either. No drugs or alcoholic tendencies.

Where is her money going? For one, she is in the highest income tax bracket so Uncle Sam takes almost half of her money between federal and state taxes. You know what she said to me the first time I talked finances with her? She just started saving in her 401k plan about five years ago. She didn't think she could afford a house and she couldn't imagine saving the maximum allowable contribution in her Retirement Plan.

People get to a point in their careers where financially, one must evaluate the greatest way their tax liability can be reduced. When speaking with this young lady, I stressed to her that if she began to save for Retirement alone, the money she set aside through her 401k could serve as a current year tax deduction as well. That was something she so desperately needed. A house, or a baby, or all three were great opportunities for her to save on taxes.

So how can *you* take advantage of tax breaks? Putting money aside for retirement is one good way to start. Even if you make $30,000, if you decided to save three percent of your money for retirement, two things will happen. First of all, you will save $900 each year. That $900 will be deducted from your salary earned, so instead of paying taxes on $30,000, your tax liability will be for $29, 100. It's like taking money out of your left hand and saving it in the right hand.

Secondly, you've just started accumulating assets, specifically for retirement. You are now a saver. I'm told the most difficult task in financial planning is starting. So consider this move a major step a person could make toward planning.

I can even think of another incentive. Most people in corporate America believe they are underpaid. Do you feel that way? Well, many retirement plans in corporate America promote saving with dollar for dollar or fifty cents per dollar contributed matching incentives. So if you save that same $900 a year, your company will match you by contributing an additional $900 under the dollar for dollar match plan in your retirement Plan. It's like free money. Just know you can't get it unless you save on your own. Now, you've saved $1800 in one year. You've reduced your tax liability and saved for retirement. Sounds like a win-win situation to me.

Let's talk about those houses for a moment. A house generally is the most expensive investment African Americans tend to make. It's something everyone is entitled to some point, simply from a comfort level perspective.

However, is it necessarily an asset? Let's define assets to make that determination. An asset is something that has value. When you purchase a house, usually the amount you owe can be more than what the house is worth, unless you purchase a house at a discount. Therefore the house is a liability. It very rarely becomes an asset to you. Only when the value of the house is more than the amount you owe on the house does it become an asset. And that includes the interest you pay over the fifteen or thirty year period.

So what is the benefit of owning a house? When you purchase a house, you receive a mortgage payment. That mortgage payment consists of principal and interest. In the very beginning, the interest payments are the majority of your payments. The interest you pay represents a tax deduction for most homeowners. Therefore, if someone is looking for a substantial tax deduction, they may look to purchase a home.

However, the miscalculation comes in when people begin to sell their house to buy a bigger house as their salary increases. This is not necessarily the smartest thing to do. I suggest you contact your Certified Public Accountant for advice. I do believe in home ownership. Some things are far more precious than money. The sense of ownership and the emotional component of having a place of your own override financial literacy. I believe it should.

Rich people though seem to enjoy the best of both worlds. How is it rich people don't pay taxes or they minimize their tax liability? First of all, many financially successful people are entrepreneurs who have established corporations. Corporate tax liability is dramatically different from personal tax liability. It is less expensive than our highest individual marginal tax bracket.

Secondly, within a corporation, expenses are deducted before taxes are paid to the government. Therefore, if you were to have a corporation, it could be possible the car you need to travel to meetings could be classified as an expense. The dinner tab you picked up when entertaining a client, the computer you purchased to keep your financial affairs in order, supplies you bought to maintain your office. All of these things may serve as justifiable expenses to conduct a business. Your CPA would make that determination based on the type of business you have.

So if you really wanted to minimize your taxes, take a look at what some financially successful people are doing. I can almost guarantee you they aren't paying a lot of taxes. Once again, it isn't what you earn rather it's what you keep. We too, should look to keep our money working for us.

CHAPTER 7

SAVE A PENNY TODAY

People always wonder why I do not talk about investments, especially at my seminars. Personally, I've always wanted to separate myself from the belief a financial advisor is basically a salesperson. Unless you count the sale of a financial plan, I take pride in showing almost anyone the value in that. I am an advisor, a true planner. Sometimes, I have people come into my office and the last thing they need is 100 shares of Cisco or 50 shares of Microsoft. They don't even need to systematically save $100 a month purchasing a quality blue chip mutual fund. Why not? Because they do not have any money saved anywhere at all. They are one paycheck away from eviction and if something serious were to happen, they would have to immediately liquidate that fund to gain access to cash. That leaves them very vulnerable to a possible loss of principal.

My first question to a potential new client is, "If you lost your job tomorrow, do you have three to six months emergency cash set aside?" The majority of the time, the answer is no. I then ask them, "Are you saving any money?" Again, the answer is usually no. I ask, "Are you participating in the retirement program offered on your job, do you have insurance, do you own your home?" Before determining if a client can invest, these are just a few questions that need to be addressed.

Until a plan is devised to address those issues, buying stock is not an option. I never object when a client who has not yet begun to accumulate wealth wants to invest. I simply devise a plan that will take care of both their short-term needs and their long term desires.

I don't want any of my clients to need money and be subject to market risk and potential loss when an emergency arises. The loss of money in the stock market affects people emotionally and often cripples their behavior when they should be saving. This is why it is very important to understand the basic fundamentals of the stock market overall. No one ever said the market only goes up. Clients must understand that a Financial Advisor cannot guarantee results nor can they guarantee a client absolutely cannot lose any money.

However, giving your investments an opportunity to grow with time can benefit you financially over the long term. As a matter of fact, the stock market has historically been one of the greatest investments available. Therefore, we must be in the position to allow our money fluctuate with market conditions and not rely upon our investments when we have emergencies.

The key is timing.

There is major value in saving and investing at an early age. However understand there is also a difference between the two.

Generally, one would set up a savings plan. Then a decision is made to strategically accumulate assets systematically. Within a savings plan, stocks, bonds, and mutual funds can be used as a viable option to utilize. The investments are choices that you have.

There are short term and long- term investments. When saving to accumulate the necessary resources for the short term, you are looking at vehicles like cash and cash equivalents such as money-market funds or CD's. Short-term investments usually can be liquidated into cash within a year without the possibility of loss to the principal amount.

Because we don't fully understand short-term investments, we tend to think a long-term investment is one to two years, if that long. However when you're seriously putting money away, a long-term investment should be money set aside for an extended period of time given the opportunity to grow. Then a chance to invest in stock, bonds, and mutual funds can arise. Individually, you must make the decision which vehicle suits you the best based on your risk tolerance, but again, that is why advisors are necessary.

The benefit to starting early, of course, is your money has a longer time to grow. Time adds the greatest value to your investments. You can put aside $100 monthly in a blue chip mutual fund earning 10% interest from the age of 21 until the age of 30. If on your 30th birthday you did not add another dollar, you would have accumulated $17,789.11. By the age of sixty, that money would have accumulated to $310,409.34. For someone who began to save at the age of 30, even if they saved $100 per month earning 10% interest in that same blue chip mutual fund until the age of 45, they would have $41,621.95 on their 45th birthday. By the age of 60 they would ultimately have $173,865.21. Can you see the value in starting early?

Some of us are somewhat knowledgeable about investments. Therefore, we set up a savings plan and committed to putting our money in the stock market. Yet we don't open our statements when they come in the mail. This is our responsibility as well, but it is a major problem in the African American community.

I have several clients that when I have an initial consultation, I request statements from them. I'm generally looking for Retirement assets, 401k Plans, bank statements, and Securities Accounts. Many of them made choices in their 401k plans when they first started the job. After being on the job four or five years, they haven't thought to evaluate their portfolio. They don't take time to review their statements but they are consistently contributing to the investments. People should use their quarterly statements sent to them by their employers as an opportunity to evaluate their financial status. How do you know if your portfolio needs adjustments if you don't even open the envelope?

Furthermore, how can you get upset with an advisor when you're not even watching your own assets? I can't begin to tell you how many portfolio evaluations I've completed and had to call the new client and say, "I'm sorry, this stock is worthless."

Although it took some time for the stocks to devalue, the client chose to ignore their money despite news heard on TV and the radio that the market was down, hoping things would change, or go away. Something did go away, their assets.

Recently I contacted a client to discuss her portfolio with her. She was well diversified but her portfolio was suffering along with the rest of the market. After the market began to improve slightly, I wanted to reiterate that her portfolio suited her risk tolerance and there was no need to make adjustments at that time. While speaking with her she stated she hadn't looked at her statement for the last several months. I realized she represented many clients out in society today. I speak to the individual at least once a month. She is always fully aware of where she stands financially, yet she still did not open her account statements.

People sometimes misunderstand their relationship with an advisor. I don't know too many advisors that say they will watch your portfolio and you don't have to do anything. It is a relationship, a mutual responsibility. If your advisor doesn't call you, you call them. Don't just let your money go down the drain and then say the advisor didn't advise. I also know of cases where advisors will contact their clients and the clients don't call back because they believe the advisor is just looking to make a trade. How would you know if you don't respond to the advisor's call? If you feel you only hear from your advisor when the advisor needs to make money, then you shouldn't be with that person. Find someone who is concerned about your financial future. But do something…take action.

The best way to do this is to first be aware of what's going on with your money and your own habits. This allows you to discern for yourself what changes might need to be made.

When in a relationship, do you know if you are a spender or a saver? What about your mate? Did you take the time out to ask? Or are you going to learn that information once you're married with children?

People often ask me how should they approach a conversation with their significant other about money. It is such a very sensitive subject. While I agree one should tread lightly, understand this…if you're building a life with someone you need to know what you are getting yourself into. The last thing you want is to have someone who is not interested in accumulating wealth. That person might not be capable just yet, but at least you should know if they're even interested in moving up financially in the world. Once you make that determination, you must evaluate each other's spending habits.

For example, if Michelle knows Derrick tends to overspend when cash is available, Michelle could avoid financial distress by reducing Derrick's available spending cash. Or, let's say Derrick pays all of his mandatory monthly bills. However, he doesn't save a penny. Michele can support Derrick by setting up a savings plan and masking it or categorizing it as a bill. Derrick's new bill is his savings. Derrick is now accumulating assets.

But here's another scenario. Michelle has a passion for the shoe store. She is at the point where she is hiding shoes from Derrick. What can Derrick do to support Michelle's desire to shop without compromising their joint commitment to save and invest? Together they can determine how many trips Michelle can make to the shoe store. For example, Michelle agrees to go to the shoe store four times a year to purchase a maximum number of five pairs of shoes each trip. They have now created a budget. Michelle will begin to look forward to her shoe shopping excursions. Her desire to shop was not eliminated. She just curtailed her trips. Now she can save additional money.

There are even more inspiring reasons peoples should begin saving. Many people are committed to tithing in their local church, which is giving 10% of everything you generate back to God. Imagine if you began saving 10% of your income in addition to tithing. Very often, I use that as a blueprint when I speak to different organizations. The Scriptures states if you bring your tithes and offerings to the storehouse, God will pour out a blessing you won't have room enough to receive. The vehicle you choose to use to save can be blessed. Not all churchgoers support this ideology.

Once I gave a seminar to a local Parent Teacher Organization in East Orange, New Jersey commenting that if you can tithe 10%, you can save an additional 10% as well. I spoke about my commitment to tithing and shared some ways that God blessed me. I also said investing could very well be an excellent vehicle that could allow us to see how the mighty hand of God could bless our investments. After the seminar was over however, a woman approached me because she was distressed that I stated we are responsible for saving for our future. She said I didn't have faith God would bless my tithes and my commitment to saving indicated I felt the need to supply my own needs.

I realized people actually feel that way but would God have us to be ignorant or unprepared? I firmly believe He will not bless you if you're not capable of handling the blessings. He will give you everything you need, including the proper management skills to maintain and appreciate the blessings. He will even give you a plan and people to help you along the way. Even people like me. The seed of information you need to save is all here but God is not going to allow money to fall out of the sky into your living room. He is capable, but I doubt if that would happen.

While giving another seminar at a woman's ministry, a young lady stated she was taught to save using a 10-10-80 agenda. Pay 10% tithes to God first. Secondly, pay yourself 10%. Finally, the remaining 80% is designated for your expenses. If 80% cannot cover your expenses, you are living beyond your means. Plant the seed, save a dollar today.

CHAPTER 8

SO YOU WANT TO RETIRE?

One potential client approached me who had been working in corporate America for the last thirty years and was concerned about their retirement plans. Because of the state of the economy, many major corporations have been offering their long- term employees an early retirement incentive. One reason for this trend is because if a client has worked for a company for at least thirty years, the expense of their salary and benefits is probably the same as two recent graduates at any average college. If the company retired the long tenured employee, they could reduce their expenses and still maintain quality service.

At any rate, my client's employer offered a generous severance package and a pension. The client was fifty years old and walked away with a pension worth approximately $300,000. The client wanted to know if I could help because it was their desire not to work anymore. However, they were accustomed to a lifestyle of approximately $50,000 a year. The $300,000 was all they had. They did not take advantage of the option to invest in a 401K plan until approximately five years before they retired and they had an outstanding loan against the monies that were accumulated. I was very disheartened when the client began to realize their co-workers that were accepting the deal were walking away with an average of $900,000 in the 401k added to the pension received by the company. The client then understood the lost opportunity. Sadly, I showed several possibilities and ultimately the client realized, at some point, they might be forced with the necessity of finding part time employment. However, we were able to compromise so the client could stay in retirement for several years before having to make that decision.

We never think about retirement until it's too late but for entrepreneurs especially, it is even more detrimental to make sure proper plans are in place. If you step out on faith and establish your very own business, there are responsibilities you face that people working for corporate America don't face. As a self- employed person, you must establish your own retirement plan.

People however tend to concentrate so much on their particular business, they don't address issues like life or health insurance and retirement planning. It's easy to let it slip through the cracks as you try to run a business. It all seems like so much work. How do you even get started? How do you decide which plan is most appropriate for you? All of that must be determined based on the financial state of your business, the stability of your income, how many employees you have, and how much you are willing to contribute on the behalf of those employees. The availability of retirement plans are many, but those questions will identify what plan you should begin to look at.

For example, if you are a sole practitioner without any employees, you might consider a Simplified Employee Pension, or Sep IRA. A Sep IRA is an employer retirement plan that uses IRAs as the funding vehicle. You have the option of putting away more money than allowed in a standard IRA.

If you have employees, and they are willing to contribute, yet your company is very small, you may look at a SIMPLE IRA or a Profit Sharing Account. If your business expenses are somewhat stable and you want to maximize your contributions, you may consider a Money Purchase Plan. As you can see, because of the many plans available, your Certified Public Accountant and your Financial Advisor would be the best people to better explain the different plans and assist you in determining which plan is for you.

How important and immediate a need is it to save for retirement? Have you ever seen a bitter old man working at

Target or Walmart grumbling to himself about the mess other people leave behind for him to clean up? He's following people everywhere they go grumbling at the mess they are making realizing that he will be the one responsible for cleaning it up. That is a clear example of someone who now must work because he did not properly plan for his retirement. Perhaps, he did not take advantage of saving in small increments when given the opportunity. Despite the thirty years of his life he had given to his company, he still has to continue to work at another company just to make ends meet. So he grumbles and mumbles complaining, upset because he has to be there. He does not have a choice.

In that very same store is a beautiful, grandmotherly figure looking fabulous. She is working the cash register or stationed at the customer service line. She always has a smile on her face and advice for the young teenagers working there as well. You'll usually find her telling the girls, "Stay away from that boy, he's no good, your skirt is much too short or your shirt is too tight, stay in school," and things of that nature. She is someone who chooses to be at that establishment. When she is ready to visit her grandchildren for a month, she can just pick up and go. The woman is working simply because she is looking for something to do. Getting out of the house and around people makes her stay young at heart and she still feels productive. This is the example of someone who properly planned for her retirement. Now what position do you want to be in? Do you want to be the bitter old man or the nice little grandmotherly figure?

Do you know when you want to retire? What does retirement mean to you?

I began thinking those questions after turning thirty. I truly believe once people hit the 'Big 3-0' they begin to concentrate on their accomplishments. They begin to evaluate their lives. Are they where they thought they would be at this stage of their lives? Are they happy with their careers? Are they financially secure?

At the age of thirty, so many major life decisions are made. People change careers, settle down, start a family, get insurance, begin saving and investing. But they also need to think about retirement. When I hit thirty, I decided I wanted to be capable of retiring by the age of 45.

Therefore, I had to make commitments toward things I needed to do to accomplish that goal. The first thing I evaluated was the type of lifestyle I want to live during retirement. Once that was done, I could put a dollar amount to that desire and have a tangible goal to work toward. It is never too early or too late to decide how you want to spend your retirement years. Whatever you decide is totally up to you.

However, I encourage you to think about it now, whether you are 25 or 55. What type of lifestyle do you want to maintain and how soon? People are living a lot longer these days. So you must understand it is to your advantage to begin saving today to plan for those days. If you really want to retire financially secure, the best way to achieve that goal is to save a little money each paycheck. The consistent contributions over an extended period of time work in your favor. Also remember if you are accustomed to surviving off of $50,000 annually, you want to save enough money during your working years to support the lifestyle you've developed for yourself.

CHAPTER 9

ESTATE PLANNING

Nobody likes to talk about death. Therefore most people avoid talking about estate planning because they don't want to think about what will happen when they die. It is a subject that should be approached sensitively. But it should be approached. Think for a moment. When you were a senior in high school, was there a death that really shattered the feelings of your graduating class? Years later, when you turned 25, how many of your old classmates are no longer around.

It seems every time you turn around you see the evidence proving African Americans are dying younger and younger.

Look at Aaliyah, Biggie Smalls, Tupac, Lisa "Left Eye" Lopez. The list goes on and on. At the age of thirty, some of your friends and associates are now even passing away due to natural causes, and health related issues. It's not just accidents anymore. So when is the right time to start planning for what will happen when you make the transition when you know tomorrow is not guaranteed?

Years ago, when my husband and I were planning to go away, we thought about the well being of our children. It was actually the first time we were going away without them and we were traveling on a plane. I started to think about who I would want to take care of my children if something ever happened to me. I have three sisters that I grew up with. I am the second oldest. My oldest sister is two years older than me. While, my two younger sisters are nine years apart. Jesse and I made the decision when my baby sister turned eighteen we wanted her to be the guardian of our two children, God forbid should something ever happen. We realized it was a big responsibility but we knew she would have the love and support she needed from the rest of the family.

We based our decision on how are children are treated now. When my son goes to Grandma's house, I can send him with homework. But, homework cannot be done at Grandma's house. That's Grandma's time and Jesse is there to be spoiled, not to be disciplined. Don't send your kids to Grandma if they have a project. My older sister lives out of town and away from the rest of the family.

Now Auntie Sonji, my sister who is closest to me in age, is the get up and go auntie. As long as she has transportation, when she rolls out, everyone rolls out. Don't even think about sending homework. Now she'll make him to it, but she won't check it. Therefore, my son knows if he spends five minutes reading, Auntie won't question him. Auntie Sonji's position is, "You should have done your homework at home. Get it-HOME WORK. Work to be done at your house, not mine."

Finally, the baby of the family, Auntie Tanya will allow you to have your fun, but homework must be done first. As a matter of fact, if Jesse isn't doing well school, he can't even go to her house. When he does bring homework to the house, she wants to see the finished product. And her standards are similar to ours.

In addition, our lifestyles are similar. She, like my children, prefers to be dressed in the latest Donna Karan, FUBU or whatever the style would be. With her I know my children would grow up with the same things they have become accustomed to. Furthermore, I know their college needs would be taken care of as well. It would not become an option for my children, but a mandate as I have. This is the aunt that would be capable of handling a financial windfall and would not squander the money away.

Consider the people in your family. Everyone has that crazy brother or aunt. You know you would not leave your children with them while you're alive. But without a will in place that could very well happen. Do you want the court system to make that decision for you? They will if you don't appoint a guardian for your small children through your will. You take that choice away.

It is also important that you review your will-substitute policies such as insurance, Retirement Plans, and 401k plans at least annually. Situations and circumstances change periodically. People get married, people get divorced, and people die. You are creating a bigger headache for your loved ones if you do not review your decisions on occasions. Your children, in five or ten years, could become adults during that time span and you can leave the money to them.

Completing an estate plan serves another important purpose. Importance does not lie in the amount of money you have accumulated during your lifetime. Knowing this I called my mother one day to ask if she had any precious heirlooms she wanted a particular daughter to have. At first she joked that she had a medal box full of problems with my name on it. I guess that was her way of saying I gave her a headache during her lifetime so she will give me a headache from the grave. She later revealed she had several outstanding projects she wanted me to finalize.

Additionally, she has a bookcase very special to her made by one of her deceased brothers. He made it when he was in the seventh grade and her father cherished the shelf until he passed away. My mother made it her business to go to Granddaddy's house to pick up the bookcase before it was damaged and has enjoyed it for at least twenty- five years and counting. She told me she wants someone who she knows will take good care of the bookcase to take possession of the property after her death. She has decided that my son, Jesse, should be that individual. Now, the bookcase probably does not have any monetary value, but it is precious and dear to my mother. The best way to ensure that Jesse receives the bookcase at my mother's death is for her to put the request in her will. How could we have known about her special bookcase if we didn't take the time to ask?

Identifying who you want to have certain items in a will also eliminates the scavenger hunt that is sure to take place after the funeral. My mother has always stated never wants to see her daughters fighting amongst each other. She just wanted us to love each other. Or at least pretend until she was gone. Now, we are all very close, but we would still fight over my mother's assets.

Although I know my family would not take it personal at the end of the day, how many people do you know aren't speaking to family members after a loved one has passed away? People have major fallouts at funerals because the house was raided or items came up missing. I'm not saying people won't be disappointed by certain decisions, but at least everyone would know clearly what the deceased wanted others to have.

Finally, we share money with relatives without understanding the consequences to our actions. Well, what do I mean? Recently, a client received a lawsuit settlement from an unanticipated death of a family member. The rightful owner of the settlement decided to share the wealth with her children. I explained several options to this young lady. The first option was that she could give a stated dollar amount without regard for taxes each year. It is classified as an annual exclusion. However, the attorney gave her the option of having the settlement paid to the children directly and she preferred that option.

I wanted to be sure she understood the money now rightfully belongs to the children and that is what she wanted. The children deposited the money *back* into the mother's account to clear the assets. Unknowingly, the children had gifted the money back to the mother, which technically gave them no rights to the money.

Subsequently, a potential problem existed in that option. When you transfer assets to someone else's name, you are giving them a gift. If that gift exceeds the annual exclusion amount, you are responsible for informing Uncle Sam that you are making a substantial gift. Every individual is entitled to a lifetime credit available to offset gift and estate taxes. The credit allows the individual to give away up to $1,000,000 worth of property during life free of gift tax or to transfer up to $1,000,000 worth of property at death, free of estate tax.

Therefore, if the mother were to give away $200,000 during her lifetime beyond her annual exemptions, she would still have $800,000 to give away at death without being subjected to estate tax. The gift excludes the spouse because property transferred to a spouse during life or death generally passes free of gift and estate tax. Any tax liability can be offset. In this case, applying the credit given to the mom and informing Uncle Sam of her intentions could eliminate any potential discrepancies. The mother decided to give the money back but complications can still arise with the continual transferring of assets.

How does this relate to estate planning? When a person is deceased a final tax return must be filed. If you accumulate substantial assets and you don't take advantage of estate planning, you could pay taxes in excess of 45% even in your death. Therefore, a great portion of the money accumulated during your lifetime can be paid to Uncle Sam, not your beneficiaries, without proper planning. Insurance proceeds are included in determining your final estate tax return liability. So if you have a net worth of $300,000 and insurance policies totaling $1,000,000, you could have a potential problem. If that mom were to die today, the money mentally designated for her children will be taxable to her. Additionally, it is not the children's money. If her will leaves everything to someone else, the children are out of luck.

However, don't be hasty in trying to preserve your assets without thinking. I know many people who are not married, get a windfall of money, and transfer the assets into their joint account. You have just gifted the other party half.

Another example of hasty thinking occurs when people put assets into their children's name. Usually, they will go to a local bank and establish a custodial account classified as a Uniform Gift to Minor's account or a Uniform Transfer to Minor's account. Once money is put into a child's name, *you* have *NO* personal rights to the money. Any monies taken out of the account before the age of majority, 18 or 21, depending on which state you reside in, should be used for the benefit of the child. In more detail, the account is designed to allow a relatively simple method of making gifts to minors of certain property (securities, cash, life insurance, and annuities) without court supervision. The account is set up with an adult acting as custodian for the minor. The adult is given broad investment powers under the "prudent person" standard. The custodian has the ability to spend property *on behalf of the minor* without a court order.

People argue with me about this point all of the time. They say, "The bank is allowing me to take out the money." That's not the purpose of the account. Finally, all of the money must be given outright to the child by the age 21.

As an individual developing an estate plan, you have the opportunity to designate things that are important to you to the people who you really want to have them. You can and should do that while you are alive and well. Additionally, you want to be well informed of all decisions you make and any problems that could arise as a result. Otherwise, start turning over in your grave, calamity is about to fall.

CHAPTER 10

REVELATION

Early that Saturday morning when I began to read pages of the book originally written when I turned 30, I wasn't sure what God was trying to show me. I discovered the purpose God had for my life. It was mind blowing what poured out once I started typing. I knew I was being called to empower and educate my community about financial planning. Our issues in this area were great. I knew by the end of that year, I would have to make dramatic changes in my life. I had always known what my purpose was, but I had wasted time walking into my destiny. The first step would be to terminate my relationship in the partnership that I had been in for the last eight years. I was restless but it was through my writing that I was able to identify where to start.

Focusing on three potentially vulnerable areas within the African-American community became my concentration. The youth, the entertainment industry, and our churches became my focal point. It became clear to me if those areas were adequately impacted, a significant change could take place socially in the mindset of our culture.

To begin with the youth I had to get close to them first. I had to present my proposal to the Board of Education to get in the schools. The average Board of Education and the public school system however is often very difficult to penetrate. Sometimes even the best programs are rejected for any number of reasons. Suburban school districts were already offering their children proper money management information. Why not give our students the same opportunity to be financially sophisticated?

For me to do the will of God, especially after sparing my life, I had no choice, but find a way to infiltrate the school system, even if it was necessary to dedicate my time and expertise for free. I met with a community leader, Sergeant DeLacy Davis, who helped me get my foot in the door. By the end of one luncheon meeting, I had a commitment for the first school I would be teaching in, not an interest, a commitment. Sergeant Davis and I presented the Board of Education with a joint proposal to teach the children about Finances. Armed with the first school's confirmation, I had the ammunition I needed to target other urban district schools.

I now go into several schools once a month to teach the basic fundamentals of finances and investments. The response in the first year was so overwhelming many students in different schools approached their principals and teachers. I realized the value in the program when I began to receive phone calls from several parents requesting information about upcoming seminars. Parents are very happy their children are learning these valuable tools. Very often parents said, "I wish someone was teaching me this when I was in High School. I definitely would have made different decisions in life."

Teaching our teenagers everything they need to know about money is essential if we are ever to really get ahead. The urban school districts agenda's purpose teaches them about stocks, bonds, and mutual funds. I found it equally important to review goal setting, to talk about credit, how the economy affects the stock market, the importance of saving, and men and women's relationship with money.

Most of them appreciate learning why FICA is taking so much money out of their paychecks from the after school job. They also appreciate someone defining what FICA was. I was an adult before learning that FICA tax is the tax an employee and their employer are required to pay to the Federal government to provide for the employee's Social Security and Medicare benefits.

The benefits from the pleasure of teaching, the opportunity to watch children finish college, begin working, or create businesses will become so rewarding. Changing the attitudes of our children towards money could be different only by providing the exposure to things that will give them a choice. Teaching the concept that we don't necessarily have to be a product of our environment opens the floodgates of possibility for them. If mommy pays the rent every other month, or lives from paycheck to paycheck, her children probably will adopt those habits…unless, the chain is broken. Just think about it. Where would you be if you learned about the importance of living within your means? What if you learned about saving for retirement even at the age of 22?

Our young adults should realize that even if they save a minimal amount of money in retirement, they are reducing their current tax liability and saving to build a nest egg. Their greatest advantage to being rich is the time they have to accumulate wealth.

Parents too can play an active role in instilling these ideas in their children as well. Most people get their first job while still living at home. Therefore, an opportunity to implement a plan of action becomes available at an early age. A young adult could save money before moving out. This way compensating parents for rent makes life easier for their parents and teaches children how to exercise discipline when it comes to money. How? If the circumstance allowed, a high school graduate could choose to continue to live at home and save money for a decent place to live rather than run out and get a place that cost $800 a month. If the parents' rent averages $800 monthly, the young adult could contribute $300 to the household and save the $500. This habit will help someone build a nest egg. If continued for two years, that young adult could accumulate $12,000 in savings, not including the interest. That is enough money to move out. Also, the young adult could be disciplined to pay out that money each month. But, in order for the financially irresponsible chain to be broken, we must be taught new things.

Our youth are continually exposed to business owners that do not live in the community. They rarely see how they too can make money for themselves. Sometimes it might seem like everyone else is making money but Black folks. You have the average Chinese store, the Spanish bodega, the Laundromat, the cleaners, your favorite clothing store and other companies surrounding our neighborhoods. The only businesses minorities can clearly identify with are beauty salons, day care centers and barbershops. The beauty supply stores aren't even owned by us.

It is very important we, especially our youth, realize we are all independent money managers. You are a business. Your business might be that you are a receptionist or a dental assistant. Even if you are employed in corporate America, you must sell yourself to your potential employer and negotiate how much your compensation will be. Most people determine if they can accept a job based on their individual needs. Would you take a position that pays you minimum wage if your salary is less than the cost of the transportation to the new job? What if your paycheck only covered the cost of child- care? Our youth should begin to see, taking a position like that is not a sound business decision.

Unfortunately, the youth often get many of their perceptions of money from the hip hop and entertainment industry. TV is a powerful tool that gives certain people unmerited respect. Several of the artists in the entertainment industry have a hold on the youth simply because kids can turn on the TV and see their favorite entertainer showing off a house or driving a car that doesn't really belong to them. The myths needed to be dispelled.

I thought to get through to the children I could utilize some of my connections to influence the youth. I hosted a local origination music video show where many of our recognized artists were interviewed on my set or I was invited to their parties, and I decided my relationship with these artists could be used to my advantage. I also host a local teen talk show that deals with the youth and their issues. I decided the first thing I would do when going into a school would be to show pictures of myself with these same artists. Then I would begin to talk about the material things the artists acquired based on their newest video. Once I had their undivided attention, I could expose the teenagers to possible ways for them to obtain things important to them without having to be a rapper, singer, actor, or sports entertainer. But what I realized was I did not need a gimmick. Credit is not given to the youth. They want to know how they can be well off or financially secure. They want to have the phat cribs and the nice cars. Anyone willing to tell them how will get their undivided attention. They watch the shows "How I'm Living and Cribs". They ask the questions about financial prosperity I wish we, as adults asked long ago.

Understanding the influence that stems from the entertainment industry, I suddenly realized artists needed to be educated also. Their spending habits are often reckless and irresponsible with little or no thought for tomorrow. They too needed a plan. Being in relationship with various entertainers, I noticed most of them are not accustomed to getting a lump sum of cash. I believe that is when their income is most erratic.

Sometimes, an advance is received but that's it for the next year. So, if an artist received an advancement of $100,000, immediately taxes should be taken out. Why? If the project doesn't do well, you will not collect another penny because there aren't any monies to collect. Additionally, the advance given to the artist is designated for various expenses. Just to name a few; production of your product, video promotion, management fees, personal expenses, etc. Therefore, if the artist created a plan when they signed a contract, they would have put themselves on a budget.

If these artists were on a plan or budget, they would own their own houses, lease, finance, or outright purchase their own cars, find their own accountants and attorneys, and make different decisions. Being young and ignorant about the ways of the industry makes them vulnerable. They don't realize if the record company leases the car for you, you don't own the car. If the record company secures the mortgage for you, you don't own the home. If the record company finds your accountant or your attorney, you will pay top dollar for advice and services you probably don't need. However, if you found your own expensive accountant and attorney, at least you know they have your interest at heart.

But most importantly, entertainers must cover the costs for everything. Again, that is why the first thing that should be taken out of that money is the taxes the artist will be liable for to avoid future problems with the IRS. The time to do that is while the resources are available. Uncle Sam generally is not very patient and he wants his money right away. But too often artists' do not set aside taxes before purchasing a house and car they already could not afford. So when tax season rolls around, if the money was not set aside, where does that leave the entertainer?

Sadly, this is the beginning of the end for many entertainers. The decisions they make when they receive their first check sets the standard for how they will react to money. Wise choices and decisions will allow them to maintain a comfortable lifestyle. Shopping, spending excessive cash just to floss, and purchasing depreciable assets, will assist in one's financial downfall.

Other issues with entertainers coincide with the fast life they live. Money comes and goes. Very often an entertainer will spend, spend, spend because the checks keep coming. So the artist gets used to the checks being available. They fall into a false sense of security that they will be on top forever making significant dollars. The reality is that an artist is as hot as their last album. There is no guarantee the new album will generate the same income the last album generated. Look at Vanilla Ice, MC Hammer, Michael Jackson. Entertainers cannot make the decision to begin saving after the next album.

Consequently for them, fame comes long before the fortune comes. But knowing this, why portray having the bling, bling, and the Lexus Trucks, the Mercedes Benz, and the fly cribs if you still live in the hood and are barely making ends meet? When entertainers get the first taste of money, they often run out and put themselves immediately in debt. Why not look to set aside money for a rainy day. That's something we all need to learn and understand. But for entertainers most times a rainy day comes more often than not.

My third focal point, offering my expertise to the churches, would prove to be a totally different situation. I personally think trying to empower the church is probably one of the most difficult things to accomplish. I found the average church does not think they need empowering. The average church is perfect. Look at the state of the churches in the urban community.

Although, I am aware that it is an individual's responsibility to handle their affairs financially there are questions to consider. Should the church have a responsibility to feed the congregation spiritually and support them in their walk with God including the empowerment and security of the people? If your pastor promoted economic empowerment from the pulpit, would you listen? Is everyone in church financially secure?

I started analyzing our beliefs and noticed that people identify mostly with the scripture that states if we suffer, we will also reign with God. The truth of the matter is this. The Bible clearly indicates that if we fulfill the requirements of God's Word, we will be blessed financially and our children will be blessed financially. To me, that means we should not remain poor emotionally, spiritually, and financially. I am not passing judgment on the church but certain things must be changed. Churches somehow are in the community but closed off from the needs.

While moderating one of the teen talk shows, the youth touched on their attitude toward the churches. Their frustration lied in the fact that there is a church and a liquor store on almost every corner in one particular community. The liquor stores were opened and the churches were not. These young adults stated that if they had options, their choices might be different. They also expressed their discontent with not being heard. They believe that negative social issues can be positively addressed through peer mediation and available recreation. If they could occupy their time proactively, they would not have time to get into mischief. I would interpret that as them saying they might be inclined to enter into a church rather than go to a liquor store if the church was opened. I remember my own experiences growing up in the church. There were always things to do at church. I really enjoyed going every Friday night. On Saturdays, the church made a concerted effort to entertain the young adults growing up. I'm not saying that churches don't have those activities today but it is apparent to the youth that no one knows about it.

Similarly, how unfortunate would it be to have a goldmine of an opportunity available to the church that is never revealed? The least the church could do is listen to or review a proposal to determine if it is suitable for their particular congregation, right? And because this was something that God called for me to do, Men and Women of God would see my spirit and let me into their establishment to "do God's will", right? I couldn't have been more wrong.

Because of customs, or people not being totally committed, or members in the church who are afraid of "outsiders", Christians often overlook great opportunities.

I realized too that corporate and natural logic does not apply when people are attending church for spiritual empowerment. I had to help them see the need for what I desired to do. I knew that any approach to "church folks" needed to spiritually- based and I had to present myself as the professional and expert I knew I was. Too often in the past however our churches had difficulty in identifying expertise. I found members in the congregation generally enter into a spiritual relationship with "a professional", not a business relationship. Very often, the initial exposure people have to Financial Consultants is based on a member in the congregation being hired for a new position in the Securities industry or the Insurance industry. So the Financial Consulting trainee attempts to build a practice starting with the people they know-the members in the church. Unfortunately, the business is designed based on numbers. In order for a new recruit to keep their job, they are required to open a certain number of accounts within a stated period of time. That Financial Consultant does not have time to educate. And because they are not familiar with all facets of the market and how it works, the members are the one's who suffer the consequences. People look at the rookie advisors who don't have the experience necessary to handle their sensitive financial needs, especially in church, yet they still give them their hard earned dollars. When people do get burnt, and if it happens to be a Black financial consultant, they blame the entire Black race.

Many days I wanted to give up on the church because of the dismal response in my local community, but God just kept telling me "Nicole, you are a Minister of Finance." What am I to say to that? I would keep trying no matter what obstacle arose.

I truly believe as Christians, if we could come together as one body of Christ, then the blessings God has in store for us would be realized. But I also knew God is not going to significantly bless us, if we can't handle the blessings. Every time I got frustrated, God began to move so that I didn't get too discouraged. After dealing with that attitude, I would often question God and myself. Is this what I'm supposed to be doing Lord? So I changed my outlook regarding the church.

As a result, I decided that educating the church would be a part of my reasonable service. No strings attached, no expectations. There were too many things our people needed to know. I knew the blessings were certainly there for the receiving when we when ready but also understood the Bible when it also stated that we perish for the lack of knowledge.

Suddenly, friends in outside communities began to support me once they heard about my call to ministry. They would ask their pastor could I come into the church to give a free seminar addressing the importance of financial planning and investing.

While speaking at one particular church, I received revelation that the seminar would be the basis of even this book. Now I can go different places and be well received.

There are requirements and mandates that God places on us that we must adhere to. We are all responsible as individuals, but Christians particularly, also have a responsibility to each other. What can you do to support your sister or brother? Spiritual support, emotional support and financial support are all necessary to see any kind of improvements in our conditions. When you really think about it, it's the trick of the devil to have you so caught up in your bills and lack of financial resources making you unable to truly dedicate time to God. If you can go to church to learn how to grow spiritually, you should be able to go to church to learn how to mature financially. It might take your having to look for a new job, cutting some unnecessary expenses, or exercising your faith that God will provide. All of these things are connected and so are we, ultimately desiring the same things.

CHAPTER 11

A REASON, A SEASON,

A LIFETIME

Events occur in our lives affecting us for a reason, a season, and sometimes a lifetime. Understanding the reasons why things occur in our lives, the proper timing it takes to accomplish our desires, and the purpose or meaning we attach to our lives can shape who we are as people. My being at the World Trade Center was for a reason. I had the opportunity to be at the right place at the right time when I went to Battery Park City on September 11th. The reason why I was there was to see firsthand those provisions the wealthy had in place. It gave me a reason to promote economic empowerment within my community.

As a result of that experience, I have completely sold out for the Lord willing to do whatever he requires of me and I truly understand that everything happens for a reason. People purchase insurance for a reason. Should something happen to them, they protect their family. They also complete a will for a reason. That reason is to properly distribute their assets as they wish. Some people try to identify the reasons why certain people have entered their life. Are they in my life for a specific reason?

The Lord certainly put certain people in my life for a reason. I never really thought about my relationships until after the tragedy. There was one man in particular comes to mind. This man was running for Congress and he requested my support. I had never been involved in a political campaign on any level. Shortly after the experience several people approached me interested in running for office. Now that I have the experience in politics, it represents another way the Lord can use me. He anointed me in that position and validated me. My relationship with community leader, DeLacy Davis in East Orange, New Jersey was for a reason as well. Being affiliated with DeLacy Davis allowed me to infiltrate the educational system effortlessly and without delay. The same thing applies to my friend, Vashti Encarcion. My relationship with her helped me effectively penetrate the churches outside of my local community.

Evaluate your life. Can you think about things that happened to you that you couldn't explain? Or people who came into your life at a particular moment? What was your reaction? Did you dismiss them or did you realize everything occurs for a reason? People will often pass through your life to edify it for a moment. Knowing the particular reason sometimes enables us to accomplish the unattainable and get through the unimaginable.

Likewise, identifying the seasons, or periods in life, we experience change enables us to determine how to handle unexpected and difficult situations. So many things can happen during a season. There could be a period of time in your life that you must put your desires on hold because of responsibilities. Very often people have children and change directions of where they were trying to go with their careers. They may work at job they hate or love for a season. Parents raise their children for a season. At times we may have to identify the proper season to let go.

When I look at my life to identify several seasons, the first one that comes to mind is the year following my experience at the World Trade Center. It is my belief that during a season, you will grow as an individual. Your behavior will change and character can be built. For me, I've discovered some changes in my own life that taught me how to completely rely on God. My purpose in life had been clearly defined during this time. My willingness to understand what is required of me was exposed to me during that season. The difficult times arose as well as the enlightening times. I've had seasons in my life where financially, I was capable of saving so much money. Almost every investment I made was a good investment. I purchased every material possession one person would ever want. That represented a season of prosperity for me. Those seasons don't always last but it's amazing how many people can't take notice of the seasons when they are being blessed.

Just as people come into your life for a reason, they come sometimes only for a season as well. Have you ever had special someone who made a powerful impact in your life for a brief time? You just connected instantly. Immediately after September 11th, I tried to ignore the fact that I needed counseling. Eventually I went back to work and concentrated on my relationship with God believing whatever process of healing needed to take place would occur through fasting, praying, and studying the Word. However, during the last year, I was in a serious car accident, totaling my car, my favorite aunt passed away, and God was supplying my every need, not my wants as I was accustomed to. At some point, I sought counseling. I went to both a regular and a Christian counselor and neither worked.

Then, someone visited my church. Initially, I was really not interested in getting to know her at all. But the Lord works in mysterious ways. As a matter of fact, I remember telling her not to look at me because I felt she could look right through me. One day I asked my pastor if she could counsel me. I had some major issues hindering my overall growth. I felt comfortable with her because she didn't know me and her relationship with God was visible to me. My intense relationship and counseling period with her was for a reason and a season. During that time, I became clear about what was required of me by God. We are good friends today. But if she were to leave my life tomorrow, I am clear what my relationship with her was all about.

Finally to define a lifetime you have to know what you want to get out of it. Whether your life is about establishing financial security, setting career accomplishments, or building a family, all of those things require planning. Financially speaking, one must save to survive a lifetime. Although it may sound difficult it is not.

Since none of us know how long we will live, we must make infinite provisions. Our savings must reflect how we intend to live for many years. The earlier you start, the less money you have to contribute annually toward savings. If you begin later on in life, you are obligated to save a large amount of money annually, if you want to ensure your money will outlast you.

We all want so much for our selves and our families. I pray my marriage to my husband is for a lifetime. My relationship with my children will last a lifetime. My family and I are connected for a lifetime. But most importantly, I pray my relationship with God is a lifelong relationship. None of those things will happen without planning and work be it spiritual, emotional, mental, or physical. It cannot happen simply by wishing it so. However, we can start by identifying the reason, season and lifetime it will take to accomplish what we desire.

EPILOUGE

When I realized God called me to the ministry, it became evident everything I had accomplished in the past needed to be put on the back burner. Everything I thought identified and accurately described me, had to be stripped. I realized not only did God call me to be a Minister of Finance, but he called me to the Office of an Evangelist as well. Therefore, he was calling me to teach the gospel. To whom much is given, much is required they say.

But naturally my first reaction was "Why me Lord? This is too much." I really wanted to know why the Ministry of Finance wasn't enough. When I decided to truly seek the Lord and do what he called for me to do, I was tested almost immediately. Because I was no longer the face of the family business and a weak economy was damaging my business, my family learned firsthand how God could supply your every need.

For a long time, my needs and wants could not be clearly separated. But every time I thought I was way off the path, God showed just a little of himself to remind me his hand was in my life all along. Every day, I thought my husband's patience would wear thin. Not only was I not contributing to the house, I was working long hours at least six days of the week. To make matters worse, it seemed as if I was not supporting the family business. I jeopardized my husband's ability to provide for the family.

But because of who God called for him to be, he carried the family on his shoulders while I was in the wilderness. As a result, God began to bless him with the desires of his heart. He transformed the business in ways I would have never envisioned. That season has allowed me to strengthen my relationship with My Father.

I know who I am based on who God has called for me to be. I am committed to you, my sisters and brothers. Whatever it takes to strengthen our culture, to bring back family values, to assist people to be financially prepared for anything, and most importantly, to win souls for the kingdom, I am available.

I tell you this story for a reason. I traveled a long road to get to this place. It is my ultimate trust in God that made me change the direction of where I was going. God is telling some of you to step out on faith. That is the key to your financial freedom. What that means to you I don't know, but if you trust in the Lord, he will carry you through. God might be telling you to go back to school, apply for that new job, create a budget, and stop being irresponsible. Whatever he is saying to you, just do it!

MATHEMATICAL CALCULATIONS

Client invests $100 monthly in a blue chip fund with at rate of return of 10% for 9 years. The client begins to invest at the age 21 and ends at the age 30 with $0.00 dollars invested.

$0.00 Present Value

$100.00Payment Monthly

9 Years

10%Interest

$17,789.11 Future Value

Client stops contributing $100 monthly in a blue chip mutual fund. They allow the money to grow from the age 30 until the age 60 with a rate of return of 10%.

$17,789.11Present Value

$0.00Payment Monthly

30Years

10% Interest

$310,409.34 Future Value

Client invests $100 monthly in a blue chip fund with at rate of return of 10% for 15 years. The client begins to invest at the age 30 and ends at the age 45 with $0.00 dollars invested.

$0.00Present Value

$100.00Payment Monthly

15Years

10%Interest

$41,621.95 Future Value

Client stops contributing $100 monthly in a blue chip mutual fund. They allow the money to grow from the age 30 until the age 60 with a rate of return of 10%.

$41,621.95Present Value

$0.00Payment Monthly

15Years

10%Interest

$173,865.21 Future Value

About the Author

Nicole B. Simpson is a Certified Financial Planner ® and Financial Advisor with over twelve years in the Securities industry. Primarily a Financial Consultant with an extensive operational background, she specializes in comprehensive financial planning that includes, but is not limited to portfolio management, establishing and maintaining Retirement accounts for small business owners and people in the entertainment industry, assessing tax exposure and limiting potential tax liabilities through utilization of various strategies.

Nicole and her husband, Jesse work together at JeSEMAN Entertainment named after their two children, Jesse and Emani. Their company founded Generation X Community Association. Through the association, Nicole educates the youth in urban areas about the basic fundamentals of financial planning and investing. She dedicates her time to being an advocate for teenagers and young adults. Nicole hosts and moderates the teen talk show titled "The X Factor" and is the former host of "Club Video Expo". Her husband and she produces, directs, and promotes "The Hot Picks @ Six and the Midday Mix on WRSU 88.7 FM each week.

Finally, Nicole accepted the call of ministry on her life and is

a member of Imani Christian Fellowship Church in New Jersey

where her family currently resides.